PARTY POPS!

PARTY POPS!

Frozen summer treats
with and without alcohol

JASSY DAVIS

THUNDER BAY
P · R · E · S · S

San Diego, California

Thunder Bay Press
An imprint of Printers Row Publishing Group
10350 Barnes Canyon Road, Suite 100, San Diego, CA 92121
www.thunderbaybooks.com • mail@thunderbaybooks.com

Thunder Bay Press
Publisher: Peter Norton
Associate Publisher: Ana Parker
Editor: Dan Mansfield
Senior Product Manager: Kathryn C. Dalby

Produced by HarperCollinsPublishers
Editor: Helen Rochester
Designer: Louise Evans
Author: Jassy Davis
All images Shutterstock

Library of Congress Control Number: 2020931718

ISBN: 978-1-64517-269-7

Printed in Latvia

24 23 22 21 20 1 2 3 4 5

INTRODUCTION

ONCE UPON A TIME IN AMERICA...

...on one cold night a boy named Frank Epperson made himself a soda and then forgot to drink it. It was 1905 and he was eleven years old, living in California, and too busy playing to remember to finish the drink he'd mixed himself. Back then, sodas were made by stirring a flavored powder into water. Frank abandoned his half-drunk glass with the wooden stick still in it and left it on the porch, only remembering about it the next morning. When he picked it up, he discovered that the drink had frozen solid. Somehow Frank managed to ease the ice out of the glass, using the stick as a handle, and that day he became the first person to ever lick an ice pop.

Frank carried on making ice pops for his friends, but more as a hobby or sideline than as a job. It wasn't until he served up a tray of ice pops at a local fireman's ball in 1922 and saw the sensation they caused that he thought there could be money to be made in these frozen treats.

He started off selling ice pops around his neighborhood, calling them "Epsicles"—a portmanteau blending of his surname and the word "icicle." His kids weren't fans of this branding; they'd already come up with their own name: Pop's 'Sicles. Deploying the kind of campaigning that only determined children can manage, they eventually persuaded him to change the name, and Epperson set up America's first Popsicle stand at the Neptune Beach amusement park on San Francisco Bay in 1923.

It didn't take long for the rest of the country to learn about ice pops, so Popsicle Corporation concessions soon opened in amusement parks and beaches across the United States. People loved them. One stand at Coney Island sold 8,000 Popsicles in just one day.

In June 1924, Frank applied for a patent for his Popsicle process. But a few months later, and in need of money, he sold his patent to the Joe Lowe Corporation. If Popsicles had been popular when Epperson was making them, under Joe Lowe they became a national craze.

Even the Depression couldn't slow Popsicles down.

To keep Popsicles affordable, Lowe came up with the two-handled Popsicle, a five-cent ice pop that two kids could share.

But it wasn't all smiles in the world of ice pops. Epperson may have patented his icy invention, but he hadn't been the only one selling ices on a stick in the 1920s. In 1922 Harry Burt of Youngstown, Ohio, had patented the manufacturing process for chocolate-covered ice-cream bars on a stick. He called them Good Humor bars and sold them from a fleet of ice-cream trucks. Meanwhile in Texas, in 1925 the M-B Ise Kream Company launched a range of fruit-flavored Frozen Suckers on sticks. The advertising campaign called them "the greatest treat you ever tasted"—and from the way they sold, it seems like the public agreed.

From 1924 to 1929 these three companies—and a few others—tussled with each other through the courts, suing and countersuing over who had the legal right to make and sell ice pops. A wary truce was eventually called, with Good Humor retaining the right to sell "ice creams, ice custards, and the like," while Popsicle held sway over "flavored syrup, water ice, or sherbet frozen on a stick." M-B Ise Kream's suppliers, Citrus Products, became co-agents for Popsicle with the Joe Lowe Corporation, and for a while people could buy Popsicle–Frozen Suckers until the name was shortened again, back to Popsicle.

There were a few more legal skirmishes over the years—especially when Popsicle tested the water by launching a Milk Popsicle in 1932. These days peace is guaranteed, as Unilever owns both the Good Humor and Popsicle brands, so there's no infighting allowed. And there's none needed either, when two billion Popsicles are sold every year.

THE ICE-POP LOWDOWN

Making your own ice pops is easier than you think. You don't need much in the way of special equipment, the ingredients are pretty budget-friendly, and they normally don't take more than ten minutes to make (plus freezing time, of course).

The recipes in this book are simple to follow and designed so that you can jump straight in without any prior knowledge, so you can skip this section if you like. But if you want to be a bit of a nerd about getting your ice pops just right, here are some things to remember.

Texture

Unlike ice creams and sorbets, ice pops are not churned, so they have a crisp, icy texture that melts in your mouth. Even those made with a dairy mix will have a firm, biteable texture. But you don't want your ice pops to be too crunchy; the faster you freeze them, the smoother the texture will be. This is down to the size of the ice crystals that form while the pop freezes.

A slow freeze creates big ice crystals, and sometimes these clump together as the pop sets, creating a hard, bland middle while all the flavor and sweetness is pushed out to the edge of the ice pop. To keep your pops smooth and evenly flavored, make sure the mixture is cool when you freeze it, and set your freezer to its lowest temperature or turn on the flash-freeze feature. The bottom of your freezer is normally the coldest part, with the back of the bottom shelf or drawer the very coldest. Freeze your ice pops there—and don't keep opening the door to check on them while they freeze. As the saying goes, a watched ice pop never freezes. Or, at least, it doesn't freeze that well.

One other thing that will affect the texture of your ice pop is adding alcohol. Alcohol has a lower freezing point than syrups, fruit juices, and dairy, and your kitchen freezer is unlikely to hit it. Ice pops made with alcohol will have a softer texture than liquor-free versions. Boozy poptails also melt faster, so be ready to be dripped on if you're not a quick eater.

Flavor

The freezing process can have a funny effect on flavors—some become stronger, some are diminished. One flavor that fades in the freezer is sweetness, which is why you need a surprising amount of sugar to make a truly sweet ice pop. If you want to get that sugary hit, the mixture should taste sweeter than seems sensible in its liquid form. Once it's frozen, that sweetness will mellow out.

Spices, on the other hand, tend to taste stronger when they're frozen. If you're infusing a simple syrup with spices (see page 15 for the how-to), don't add too many and don't let the flavors infuse for too long.

Another flavor that gets dialed up during freezing is alcohol. Whether it's the sharp heat of vodka, the earthiness of tequila, or the botanical richness of gin, you will taste it quite strongly in your finished ice pops. You might think that the orange juice and sugar syrup will hide the roughness of the cheap bottle of vodka left over from last night's party, but it really won't. If you wouldn't drink it from a glass, don't freeze it onto a stick.

When it comes to the fresh ingredients, use the best quality you can afford. If you're blending fruits into the mixture, make sure they are ripe. You can brighten the flavors in your ice pops with a squeeze of lemon or lime juice. A small pinch of salt also has the same effect.

TOOLS FOR THE JOB

To make ice pops, the main pieces of kitchen equipment you need are a large bowl, a spoon, and some sort of mold to freeze them in. For plenty of recipes, this is all the equipment you will need, but there are a few extras that can help.

Blender
A good-quality blender is useful for pureeing fresh fruits with syrups and juices.

Juicer
A sturdy juicer will cut the time and mess in half when you're squeezing citrus fruits.

Saucepan
For making simple syrups and for simmering together mixes that benefit from a bit of heat infusion, like mulled wine or spice-infused milk.

Fine-mesh sieve
To strain mixtures. Especially useful if you want to make clear ice pops without the cloudiness that fruit pulps can create.

Kitchen scales, measuring cups, and spoons
Digital scales can make measuring out ingredients easy—just put your mixing bowl on them and start pouring in the ingredients. Measuring cups and spoons are another option for weighing out ingredients. The ingredient weights in the book are given in ounces.

Pitchers and ladles
Transferring the liquid mix into the molds is easier if you use a pitcher with a spout or a small ladle.

Molds and sticks

There are lots of ice-pop molds on the market, and even some pop makers that will shape and set your ice pops in under an hour. To test these recipes, I used a mixture of soft silicone molds and rigid plastic molds, all around 4 fl. oz. per ice pop.

As a rule of thumb, I found that fruit- and syrup-based ice pops froze really well in the silicone molds, while the dairy-based pops tended to do better in a hard-sided plastic mold, especially if they had alcohol in them. If you do make a cream version in a soft mold and the mold is unwilling to let it go—even after you've dipped it in warm water— carefully insert a thin, round-bladed knife and run it around the edge of the ice pop to loosen it. It should pull straight out.

You don't have to buy special molds to make ice pops—you can use freezer-proof shot glasses; tall, thin glasses; ice cube trays; or disposable cups. Don't use anything too wide, though, like a tumbler or a bowl, as the ice pops can end up too thick, which slows down the freezing process and makes them too icy. Also remember that the stick has to be able to hold up the ice pop—making a giant ice pop looks like fun until you unmold it and realize the only way you'll be able to eat it is from a bowl with a spoon and chisel.

Most molds come either with stick holders (little slits cut into the mold lid that will hold the sticks snugly in place) or with plastic sticks set into individual lids. If you buy a mold that doesn't come with integral sticks, wooden sticks are the best option. They are inexpensive and your ice pops will cling firmly onto them.

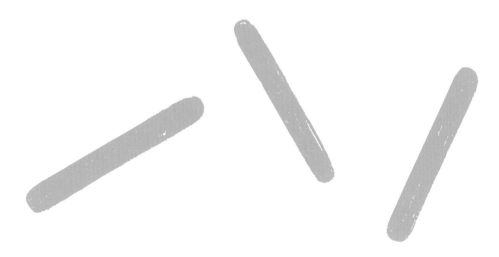

TRICKS & TECHNIQUES

Get ahead on the ice pop–making process with these smart skills that will help you elevate your game.

Cooling your mix

When you're making ice pops, you want the mixture to be at least room temperature, if not colder, to make sure the freezing process doesn't take too long. If you're making ice pops with a simple syrup or with a heat-infused mixture and don't want to wait hours for it to cool down, you can speed up the process by using an ice bath. Fill your sink or a large bowl with plenty of ice, add a little cold water, and set a wide bowl on top. Pour the hot liquid into the bowl and stir it for a few minutes. Leave the mixture for around 1 hour, stirring every 15 minutes, until it's cold and ready for freezing.

Filling your molds

When you're adding your mixture to the mold, don't fill it right to the brim. You need to leave space for the ice pops to expand as they freeze. Around ¼ inch should be sufficient.

Freezing your ice pops

Set your freezer to its coldest setting and clear out a space on the bottom shelf so the molds can sit upright. Freezing times vary, but I find that fruit juice and syrup-based ice pops take around 5–8 hours to set, while dairy or coconut milk–based pops take 8–10 hours, and anything with alcohol in it is best left in the freezer for at least 12 hours to make sure it is solid.

If your molds have integral sticks in the lids, you can put your ice pops straight into the freezer and leave them until morning. If you need to insert the sticks yourself, you normally need to let the ice pops freeze a little first to thicken them up. Putting the sticks into the ice pops when they're liquid tends to result in the sticks freezing at odd angles, making the ice pops hard to eat. Sometimes ice pops made with dairy or coconut mixtures can be stiff enough to insert the sticks straight away, but for thinner mixtures, freeze them for around 2–3 hours until they're slushy—the amount of time will depend on how cold your freezer is and whether the pops contain alcohol or not. When they're slushy, take the ice pops out of the freezer, insert the sticks, and return the molds to the freezer.

Layering your ice pops

If you want to freeze different flavors in different layers, freeze the first layer in the mold for 2–3 hours until it's quite thick but still slushy. Don't freeze it until it's solid—you still need to be able to get the stick in. Once your first layer is thick, pour in the next layer, insert the stick, and freeze again for the same amount of time, until thick. For a third or fourth layer, repeat the process.

Adding stripes

If you're making an ice pop with a thick, dairy-based mixture and a fruit puree, it can be fun to swirl them together to make stripes. Layer the two mixtures in your mold in alternate layers, then stir a knife or skewer through the mixture a couple of times to mingle them together. Insert the sticks and freeze.

Suspending ingredients

Adding chunks of chocolate or fruit to a liquid mixture normally results in the solid ingredients drifting to the bottom of the mold. The best way to make sure your chocolate chips and fruit chunks are evenly spread through the ice pop is to pour half the mixture into the mold, freeze for 2–3 hours until slushy, then gently drop in the ingredients, insert the sticks, and freeze until set.

Unmolding your ice pops

Patient ice-pop makers can let their frozen treats sit in their molds at room temperature for a couple of minutes, then easily pull them out. For a quicker unmolding, fill a large bowl or sink with warm water (hand-hot is warm enough), then dip the molds into the water for between 10 and 30 seconds. Check every so often to see if the ice pops are ready to come out. If the stick comes out by itself, the ice pops have gotten too soft and need to go back into the freezer to reset.

Storing your ice pops

The best way to store your ice pops is in the molds, but that's not always practical if your molds are attached in one big block. If you're unmolding a batch of ice pops in one go but aren't eating them right away, wrap them in parchment paper and store in freezer bags.

If the edges of the ice pops are too soft when you unmold them, you can freeze them a second time to set the shape. Line a baking sheet with parchment paper, lay the unmolded ice pops on the sheet, and freeze for 30–60 minutes until solid. Don't leave them in the freezer overnight like this—they can start to develop freezer burn or pick up the flavors of other foods stored in the freezer. Once your ice pops are set, wrap them individually in parchment paper and pop them into freezer bags.

Ice pops are best eaten within one week, but they will keep well enough in the freezer for up to a month.

THE SWEET STUFF

You can use all sorts of sweeteners in ice pops—cane sugar in all its forms, maple syrup, honey, agave syrup, or even sweeteners like Xylitol or Stevia. A lot of the recipes in this book use simple syrup—a mixture of sugar and water boiled together to make a clear syrup. I like it because it's easy to make and easy to add to mixtures; it gives the ice pops a slightly softer, creamier texture; and you can add flavors to it to enhance the ice pops.

Simple syrup also keeps really well in the fridge, so it's worth making a big batch to keep you going for a few weeks. What you don't use in pops, you could always add to cocktails (the straightforward drinking kind, rather than the frozen-on-a-stick kind). The recipe opposite can easily be scaled up or down. The ratio is very easy: equal parts sugar and water.

SIMPLE SYRUP

1 cup granulated sugar
1 cup water

Tip the sugar into a saucepan and pour in the water. Set the pan on a medium-high heat and bring to a boil, without stirring. Once the liquid is boiling, set your timer for 2 minutes. After 2 minutes, take the pan off the heat and let the syrup cool. Transfer to a clean jar or tub, seal, and store in the refrigerator for up to a month.

ADDING FLAVORS

You can add fresh herbs, dried spices, or even citrus zest to the syrup to flavor it. Herbs that work well include rosemary, thyme, bay, and mint. Just add 3–4 small sprigs to the sugar and water, then follow the recipe. When you transfer the syrup to a jar or tub, strain out the sprigs through a fine-mesh sieve.

For a spiced syrup, try infusing a cinnamon stick, a few cardamom pods, or a star anise with the syrup. For syrup with a bit of zing, add a few strips of lemon, lime, or orange peel.

THE RECIPES

ICE POPS WITH ALCOHOL

PALOMA
PALETAS

MAKES 8

The paloma is Mexico's favorite cocktail—even more popular than the margarita. A mix of sweet and sour with a salty tang from the tequila, it's a thirst-quenching and very tasty drink. It makes an elegant ice pop that I think is especially good as a pre-dinner treat.

1 cup Simple Syrup
  (see page 15)
1 cup fresh grapefruit juice
Juice of 1 lime
2 fl. oz. silver tequila
1 cup fresh ruby
  grapefruit juice

Make the Simple Syrup following the recipe on page 15, then let it cool.

Pour the regular grapefruit juice into a pitcher (keep the ruby grapefruit juice for later). Squeeze in the juice from half the lime (save the rest for later) and add 1 fl. oz. of the tequila. Add ½ cup of Simple Syrup. Stir to mix, then pour the mixture into molds and freeze for 2–3 hours until slushy and semifrozen.

Pour the remaining Simple Syrup and tequila into the pitcher. Squeeze in the remaining lime juice. Stir in the ruby grapefruit juice. Take the semifrozen ice pops out of the freezer and pour in the ruby grapefruit mixture, then insert sticks and freeze overnight until solid.

STRAWBERRY TEQUILA SUNRISE
ICE POPS

MAKES 8

These ice pops have blushing red tops, thanks to a mix of grenadine and strawberries, and a cooling orange and tequila base. If you don't have grenadine, just use Simple Syrup instead (see the recipe on page 15)—the ice pops will be pink rather than red, but just as tasty.

½ cup strawberries
½ cup grenadine syrup
Juice of 1 lime
⅔ cup Simple Syrup
   (see page 15)
2 cups fresh orange juice
2 fl. oz. silver tequila

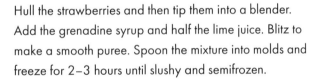

Hull the strawberries and then tip them into a blender. Add the grenadine syrup and half the lime juice. Blitz to make a smooth puree. Spoon the mixture into molds and freeze for 2–3 hours until slushy and semifrozen.

Make the Simple Syrup following the recipe on page 15, then let it cool.

Pour the remaining lime juice into a pitcher. Add the orange juice, Simple Syrup, and tequila and stir well. Pour the orange and tequila mixture into the molds on top of the strawberry mix. Insert sticks into the ice pops and freeze overnight.

BLUEBERRY SKY POPS

MAKES 6

As up, up, and away as any ice pop can be. This recipe was inspired by the Aviation, the turn-of-the-century cocktail invented to celebrate the adventures of the first pilots taking to the skies in the early 1900s. The cocktail gets its lilac-blue hue from crème de violette, but for the ice pop I thought a fruity hit of blueberry would be tastier.

½ cup Simple Syrup (see page 15)
14-oz. can coconut milk
⅔ cup blueberries
2 fl. oz. London dry gin

Make the Simple Syrup following the recipe on page 15, then let it cool.

Give the can of coconut milk a good shake to make sure the coconut cream and water are mixed together. Pour into a blender. Add the Simple Syrup and blueberries. Blitz until combined and smooth. You can add the gin and pulse again to combine, or pour the mixture through a sieve into a pitcher to catch any unblended pulp, then add the gin and stir.

Pour the coconut mixture into molds and freeze for 2–3 hours until slushy and semifrozen. Insert sticks into the ice pops, then freeze overnight until set.

CHERRY COLA
POPTAILS

MAKES 6–8

A tipsy, grown-up version of cherry cola with an extra kick of bourbon that'll take you straight back to the 1980s—shoulder pads and blue eye shadow optional.

2⅔ cups cola
Juice of 1 lime
1 fl. oz. cherry liqueur
1 fl. oz. bourbon

Pour the cola into a pitcher and let it sit for 1–2 hours so it goes slightly flat. Stir in the lime juice, cherry liqueur, and bourbon. Pour the mixture into molds and freeze for 2–3 hours until semifrozen. Insert sticks into the slushy cola, then freeze overnight until solid.

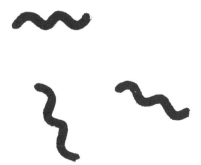

STRAWBERRY SIDECAR FREEZIES

MAKES 6–8

Put some Parisian chic into your ice pops by basing them around the Sidecar, a brandy cocktail invented in a Paris bistro and named after the motorcycle sidecar that brought a favorite customer to and from the bar.

1⅓ cups Simple Syrup (see page 15)
½ cup strawberries
1 cup fresh lemon juice
½ cup cold water
1 fl. oz. brandy
1 fl. oz. triple sec

Make the Simple Syrup following the recipe on page 15, then let it cool.

Hull the strawberries and pop them in a blender. Add the Simple Syrup, lemon juice, and water and blitz until smooth. You can add the brandy and triple sec and pulse again to combine, or pour the mixture through a sieve into a pitcher to catch any unblended pulp, then add the brandy and triple sec and stir.

Pour the mixture into molds. Freeze for 2–3 hours until semifrozen. Insert sticks into the slushy ice pops and freeze for an additional 5–6 hours until solid.

SEA BREEZER
POPS

MAKES 6-8

In the 1990s, no bar menu was complete unless it had a Sea Breeze on it. A dry mix of cranberry, grapefruit, lime, and vodka, it was the drink of the summer—every summer—until the Cosmopolitan came along to claim its crown. Turned into a tangy frozen poptail, the Sea Breeze can hold its head up high once again.

• •

1 cup Simple Syrup (see page 15)
1 cup ruby grapefruit juice
1 cup cranberry juice drink
Juice of 2 limes
2 fl. oz. good-quality vodka

• •

Make the Simple Syrup following the recipe on page 15, then let it cool.

Pour the grapefruit juice into a pitcher and add the cranberry juice, fresh lime juice, and vodka. Pour in the cooled Simple Syrup and stir to mix everything together. Pour the mixture into molds and freeze for 2–3 hours until slushy and semifrozen. Insert sticks and freeze overnight until solid.

GIN & TONIC
ICE POPS

MAKES 8

Whether you like juniper-heavy London dry gins, malty Old Toms, or botanical-rich artisanal gins, these ice pops are a must for G&T fans. The tonic water and citrus give them a crisp, zingy edge. Just add your favorite gin.

½ cup Simple Syrup (see page 15)
½ lemon, ½ lime, and a chunk of cucumber
2 tbsp. fresh lime or lemon juice
2 fl. oz. good-quality gin

Pour the tonic water into a pitcher and leave it for 1–2 hours to go slightly flat.

Make the Simple Syrup following the recipe on page 15, then let it cool.

Thinly slice the lemon and lime halves, and a small chunk of cucumber, then add a few slices of each to the molds. Stir the Simple Syrup, lime or lemon juice, and gin into the tonic water. Pour the mixture into molds and freeze for 2–3 hours until slushy and semifrozen. Insert sticks and freeze overnight until solid.

STRAWBERRY & BOURBON TWISTS

MAKES 10

A single-serve strawberry ice cream that takes five minutes to prepare and comes with a bonus hit of bourbon for vanilla richness.

½ cup strawberries
2 tbsp. fresh lemon juice
14-oz. can sweetened
    condensed milk
1 cup heavy cream
1 cup whole milk
2 fl. oz. bourbon

Hull the strawberries and then tip them into a bowl. Add the lemon juice and use a handheld blender to blitz into a puree. No blender? Use a fork to crush the strawberries and stir in the lemon juice. Set aside.

Pour the condensed milk and heavy cream into a mixing bowl and whisk together until smooth. Whisk in the milk. Add the strawberry puree and bourbon and gently stir to just combine. Use a small ladle to pour the mixture into molds, or transfer the mix to a pitcher and pour it in. Freeze for 2–3 hours until starting to set. Insert sticks and then freeze overnight until solid.

BLOOD ORANGE FROGRONIS

A Frogroni is a Negroni that's spent a few hours in the freezer. Blood oranges are a New Year's treat and the juice is brilliant blended with the mix of gin, Campari, and sweet vermouth to make a fruity version of the famous Italian aperitivo. Be careful when you're measuring out the spirits—more than 2 fl. oz. in the mix will keep the ice pops from freezing.

1 cup Simple Syrup
   (see page 15)
2 cups fresh blood orange juice
¾ fl. oz. Campari
¾ fl. oz. London dry gin
¾ fl. oz. sweet red vermouth

Make the Simple Syrup following the recipe on page 15, then let it cool.

When you're ready to make the ice pops, pour the syrup into a pitcher. Add the blood orange juice, Campari, gin, and vermouth. Stir well. For clear ice pops, pour the mix through a sieve to catch any orange pulp. Don't press the pulp to squeeze out any remaining juice—that will make the ice pops cloudy.

Pour the mixture into molds and freeze for 2–3 hours until slushy and semifrozen. Insert sticks into the ice pops, then freeze overnight until set.

PEPPERMINT
MARTINI

ICE POPS

MAKES 6–8

One way to make wrapping gifts for the holidays more fun is to
mix yourself a candy cane martini—a peppermint twist on a vodka
martini—to sip while you stick and snip ribbons and paper. Inspired
by that festive treat, I mixed up a batch of these mint and coconut
ice pops that have a snowy texture and a wintry flavor.

/////////////////// ///////////////////////////////

14-oz. can sweetened
    condensed milk
1 cup coconut milk
1 oz. coconut cream
2 fl. oz. good-quality vodka
1 tsp. peppermint extract

Pour the condensed milk and coconut milk into a mixing
bowl and whisk together until smooth. Spoon in the
coconut cream and whisk to combine. Add the vodka
and peppermint extract and whisk again briefly. Use a
small ladle to pour the mixture into molds, or transfer the
mix to a pitcher and pour in. Freeze for 2–3 hours. Insert
sticks and freeze overnight until solid.

BELLINI ICE POPS

MAKES 10

Sitting on the terrace of Harry's Bar in Venice and sipping a fresh peach Bellini has always been on my bucket list. I haven't made it there yet, but in the meantime these fizzy peach ice pops are the next best thing. When you're picking a prosecco, go for one labeled "brut," which is dry but still fresh and fruity.

• •

½ cup Simple Syrup (see page 15)
1 cup brut prosecco
14-oz. can peaches in fruit juice

• •

Make the Simple Syrup following the recipe on page 15, then let it cool.

Pour the prosecco into a pitcher or bowl and let it sit for 1 hour to go slightly flat.

When you're ready to make the ice pops, tip the canned peaches and their juice into a blender, add the Simple Syrup, and blitz to combine. Pour in the prosecco and blitz again briefly. Pour the mixture into molds and put in the freezer for 2–3 hours until semifrozen. Insert sticks and freeze overnight until set.

MOSCOW MULE
ICE POPS

The Moscow Mule was supposedly invented in the
Cock 'n' Bull Saloon on the Sunset Strip in the 1940s. It was called
"the vodka drink with a kick," and these fiery ice pops, packed
with ginger heat and vodka, will definitely get your taste
buds buzzing.

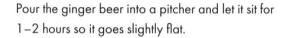

2⅔ cups ginger beer
2 fl. oz. good-quality vodka
Juice of 2 limes

Pour the ginger beer into a pitcher and let it sit for
1–2 hours so it goes slightly flat.

When you're ready to make the ice pops, add the
vodka and lime juice to the ginger beer. Stir well, then
pour the mixture into molds and freeze for 2–3 hours
until slushy and semifrozen. Insert sticks, then freeze
overnight until solid.

ORANGE & APEROL SPRITZICLES

MAKES 6

Sometime in the early 2000s, Aperol Spritzes escaped from the
Venetian bars where they're a pre-dinner essential, and started to take
over the world. Now no self-respecting bar opens up without a Spritz
on the menu. The original drink is always made with Aperol, but other
bitter Italian aperitifs, like Campari and Cynar, work just as well, and
you can swap them into this ice pop recipe, too.

1 cup Simple Syrup
   (see page 15)
1 cup brut prosecco
1 cup fresh orange juice
2 fl. oz. Aperol

Make the Simple Syrup following the recipe on page 15,
then let it cool.

Pour the prosecco into a pitcher or bowl and let it sit
for 1 hour to go slightly flat.

When you're ready to make the ice pops, add the Simple
Syrup to the prosecco and pour in the orange juice
and Aperol. Stir to mix. Pour the mixture into molds and
freeze for 2–3 hours until semifrozen. Insert sticks into
the molds and freeze overnight until solid.

ICE ICE BAILEYS

When I told friends I was writing a book of boozy ice pops, they all said the same thing: "Make one with Baileys!" So I can guarantee that all your friends will want to try these ice pops, too. There are two ways to make them: without cocoa, which gives you a straight-up, creamy, Baileys-flavored ice pop; or with cocoa, which turns the mix into an outrageously decadent frozen chocolate mousse.

2¼ cups whole milk
⅔ cup superfine sugar
2 tbsp. unsweetened cocoa powder (optional)
½ cup Baileys Original Irish Cream
Chocolate sprinkles, to serve

Pour the milk into a saucepan and add the sugar and cocoa powder, if you're using it. Whisk together until combined, then place the pan on a medium heat and bring to a gentle boil—keep your eye on it, don't let it boil over. When the milk is just boiling, turn the heat down a little and simmer for 2 minutes, stirring. Pour the hot milk into a heatproof pitcher and set aside for 1–2 hours to cool (see the tip on page 12 on using ice baths to cool your mixture quickly).

Stir the Baileys into the cooled milk. Pour the mixture into molds and freeze for 2–3 hours until thickened. Insert the sticks, then freeze overnight until solid.

To serve, unmold and scatter with a few chocolate sprinkles.

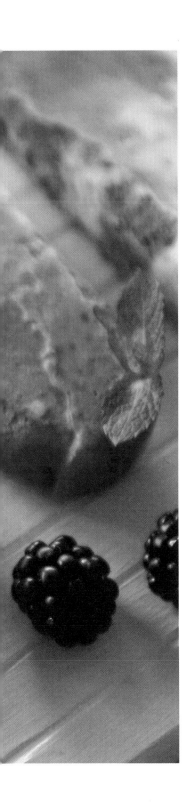

ICED
BRAMBLES

MAKES 8

The Bramble was invented in the 1980s by legendary London bartender Dick Bradsell. He was inspired by his boyhood summers spent in the countryside, picking blackberries and getting scratched by brambles. If you've been blackberrying and have more fruit than you can bake into a pie, turn a few into these simple, nostalgic ice pops.

• •

¾ cup blackberries
½ cup powdered sugar
2⅔ cups whole milk
Juice of ½ lime
2 fl. oz. London dry gin

• •

Tip the blackberries into a blender. Add the powdered sugar and pour in the milk and lime juice. Blitz until smooth and combined. Pour in the gin and pulse briefly to mix it in. Pour the mixture into molds and freeze for 2–3 hours until semifrozen. Insert sticks into the molds and freeze overnight until set.

CHERRY KIRSCH
KICKS

MAKES 10

Every June in Zug, in northern Switzerland, the Chriesigloggä
(cherry bell) rings out, marking the start of the cherry harvest.
Cherries are a big deal in Zug, where the season is celebrated with
a 300-year-old race through the old town, and a special market
that sells fresh cherries and cherry products, including a cherry liqueur
called kirschwasser. It's drier than other cherry liqueurs, so serving
kirschwasser with a small lemon ice pop makes it refreshing rather
than sweet.

〜〜〜〜〜〜〜〜〜〜〜〜〜〜〜〜〜〜〜〜〜〜〜〜〜〜〜〜〜〜〜〜

1⅓ cups Simple Syrup
(see page 15)
1 cup fresh lemon juice
⅔ cup cold water
3 oz. fresh cherries, halved
and pitted
1⅓ cups chilled kirschwasser
or cherry liqueur

Make the Simple Syrup following the recipe on page 15,
then let it cool.

Pour the Simple Syrup, lemon juice, and water into a
pitcher and stir to combine. Pour the mixture into molds.
Freeze for 2–3 hours until semifrozen, then gently press
the halved cherries into the slushy ice pops and insert the
sticks. Freeze for an additional 6–8 hours until solid.

To serve, pour a large measure of kirschwasser into
each glass, unmold the ice pops, and serve them
dunked in the kirschwasser.

RASPBERRY RUSSIAN RIPPLES

MAKES 6

In *The Big Lebowski*, the Dude drinks nine White Russians—a sticky drink made with vodka, coffee liqueur, and cream that was buried at the bottom of bar menus until the Coen brothers gave it a supporting role in their movie. To turn it into a frozen version, I added raspberries to lighten up the dairy, along with a dash of crème de cacao for a rich hint of chocolate.

∿∿∿∿∿∿∿∿∿∿∿∿   ∿∿∿∿∿∿∿∿∿∿∿∿

¼ cup Simple Syrup
   (see page 15)
¾ cup raspberries
1¼ cups heavy cream
1 cup whole milk
1 fl. oz. good-quality vodka
1 fl. oz. crème de cacao
   white liqueur

Make the Simple Syrup following the recipe on page 15, then let it cool.

Tip the raspberries into a small bowl and roughly crush them with a fork. Set aside.

Pour the cream into a mixing bowl and whisk until it starts to thicken slightly. Pour in the milk, Simple Syrup, vodka, and crème de cacao. Whisk together until smooth and combined. Gently fold in the crushed berries to just mix. Spoon the mixture into the molds, insert a stick into each mold, and freeze overnight.

STRAWBERRY FROSÉ
ICE POPS

MAKES 8–10

A frosé is a frozen rosé that's normally served as a slushy.
Keep it in the freezer overnight and you get fruity ice pops
like these.

½ cup Simple Syrup
   (see page 15)
1⅓ cups strawberries
1⅓ cups dry rosé wine
⅔ cup ruby grapefruit juice
Juice of 2 limes
A pinch of sea salt

Make the Simple Syrup following the recipe on page 15, then let it cool.

Hull the strawberries and tip them into a blender. Pour in the rosé wine, ruby grapefruit juice, lime juice, and Simple Syrup. Add a small pinch of sea salt. Blitz until smooth and combined. Pour through a sieve into a pitcher, and use the back of a spoon to press any pulp that collects in the sieve to squeeze out any remaining juice.

Pour the mixture into molds and freeze for 2–3 hours until slushy and semifrozen. Insert sticks and freeze overnight until solid.

LIME & GIN GIMLET POPTAILS

MAKES 6-8

A 50/50 mix of gin and lime cordial, the Gimlet is a cocktail that made its way around the world with the English navy, whose sailors drank it for its "medicinal" benefits. Turned into an ice pop, it's sweet and sharp with a botanical twist, thanks to the gin.

● ● ● ● ● ● ● ● ● ● ● ● ● ●   ●

1⅓ cups Simple Syrup
   (see page 15)
1 cup fresh lime juice
⅔ cup cold water
2 fl. oz. London dry gin
1 lime, to serve

Make the Simple Syrup following the recipe on page 15, then let it cool.

When you're ready to make the ice pops, pour the Simple Syrup, lime juice, water, and gin into a pitcher and stir to mix. Pour the mixture into molds. Freeze for 2–3 hours until semifrozen. Push a slice of lime into each ice pop, then insert the sticks into the slushy ice pops and freeze overnight until solid.

IRISH COFFEE PUDDING POPS

An Irish coffee after dinner is a treat on cold, wet evenings, but in the summer I want something more refreshing, which is where these indulgent ice pops come in. The raw sugar adds a touch of taffy to the mix of bitter coffee and malted whiskey.

1 cup hot coffee
½ cup raw sugar
1⅔ cups half and half
2 fl. oz. Irish whiskey
¾ cup chocolate chips

Pour the coffee into a heatproof pitcher, add the sugar, and stir until the sugar has dissolved. Set aside to cool (see the tip on page 12 on using ice baths to cool your ice pop mixes quickly).

When the coffee is cool, stir in the half and half and Irish whiskey. Pour the Irish coffee mixture into molds and freeze for 2 hours until just thickening. Sprinkle the chocolate chips into the molds and stir gently with a butter knife or skewer to mix them in. Insert sticks into the ice pops and freeze overnight until solid.

SEX ON THE BEACH
ICE STICKS

MAKES 8–10

Fun, fruity, and just a little flirty, Sex on the Beach is the essential holiday cocktail. The mix of sweet fruit juices with a kick of booze from schnapps and vodka works brilliantly in an ice pop, too.

● ● ● ● ● ● ● ● ● ● ● ● ●   ● ● ● ● ● ● ● ● ● ● ● ● ● ● ● ● ● ● ●

1 cup Simple Syrup
   (see page 15)
1 cup pineapple juice
1 cup cranberry juice
1 cup fresh orange juice
1 fl. oz. peach schnapps
1 fl. oz. good-quality vodka

Make the Simple Syrup following the recipe on page 15, then let it cool.

Pour the pineapple juice into a pitcher and add the cranberry juice, orange juice, peach schnapps, and vodka. Pour in the cooled Simple Syrup and stir to mix everything together. Pour the mixture into molds and freeze for 2–3 hours until slushy and semifrozen. Insert sticks and freeze overnight until solid.

MINTED
BOURBON
& LIME

ICE POPS

MAKES 8

A Kentucky classic, a mint julep is an excellent way to cool
down on hot and humid summer days. This frozen take on the
super-chilled bourbon cocktail is based around lime juice, which
gives these ice pops a mouthwatering sharpness sweetened by
a mint-spiked sugar syrup.

1⅓ cups minty Simple Syrup
(see page 15)
1 cup fresh lime juice
⅔ cup cold water
2 fl. oz. bourbon
A few drops of green food
coloring (optional)

Make the Simple Syrup following the recipe on page 15,
then let it cool.

When you want to make the ice pops, pour the Simple
Syrup, lime juice, water, and bourbon into a pitcher and
stir to mix. If you are using green food coloring, add
a few drops to the mix and stir in. Pour the mixture into
molds. Freeze for 3 hours until just starting to freeze.
Insert the sticks into the slushy ice pops and freeze for
another 6–8 hours until solid.

COLD FASHIONEDS

MAKES 6

Did Don Draper ever stop for an ice pop in *Mad Men*? If he didn't, it's probably because no one thought to turn his favorite cocktail—the Old Fashioned—into a frozen treat. This orange juice–based version keeps the bourbon up front, which adds a dash of brown-sugar sweetness to the intense, crisp citrus.

1 cup Simple Syrup
  (see page 15)
2 cups fresh orange juice
2 fl. oz. bourbon
A few dashes of Angostura
  bitters

Make the Simple Syrup following the recipe on page 15, then let it cool.

Pour the orange juice into a pitcher and add the Simple Syrup, bourbon, and a few dashes of Angostura bitters (4–5 good shakes should do it). Stir to mix, then pour the orange mixture into the molds. Freeze for 2–3 hours, then take the molds out of the freezer and insert the sticks into the slushy, semifrozen ice pops. Return to the freezer for 3–5 hours until solid.

CUCUMBER MARTINI COOLERS

MAKES 6–8

The nearest thing to an English country garden captured in ice-pop form. The green cucumber flavor is front and center, but if you'd like something a little more aromatic, swap the vodka for your favorite gin.

½ cup Simple Syrup (see page 15)
20 oz. roughly chopped cucumber
Juice of ½ lime
2 fl. oz. good-quality vodka

Make the Simple Syrup following the recipe on page 15, then let it cool.

Tip the cucumber into a blender. Add the simple syrup, lime juice, and vodka. Blitz until blended and smooth. For smooth ice pops, pour the mixture through a sieve into a pitcher to catch any unblended pulp. Press the pulp to squeeze out as much juice as possible. Pour the mixture into molds and freeze for 2–3 hours until semifrozen. Insert sticks into the molds and freeze overnight until solid.

STRAWBERRY & PEACH DAIQUIRI POPS

MAKES 6

A triple-decker take on the classic Caribbean cocktail that sandwiches a cool and creamy coconut layer between two fruity daiquiri twists: peach on the bottom, strawberry on top. The chia seeds add texture to the ice pops, but you can leave them out if you prefer.

For the strawberry layer:
½ cup Simple Syrup
  (see page 15)
¾ cup strawberries
Juice of ½ lime
1 fl. oz. white rum

For the coconut layer:
1 cup coconut milk
2 tsp. chia seeds

For the peach layer:
1 cup fresh peaches, pitted
  and chopped
2 tbsp. powdered sugar
1 fl. oz. white rum

Make the Simple Syrup following the recipe on page 15, then let it cool.

Hull and chop the strawberries, then tip into a blender and add the Simple Syrup, lime juice, and white rum. Blitz until smooth and combined. Ladle the strawberry puree into the molds, or transfer to a pitcher and pour it in. Freeze for 2–3 hours until semifrozen.

About 40 minutes before you want to add the second layer, pour the coconut milk into a bowl and whisk to make sure it is smooth and combined. Add the chia seeds and stir to mix. Set aside for 30 minutes to let the chia seeds expand. Take the molds out of the freezer and layer the coconut and chia seed mix into the molds. Insert the ice pop sticks and return to the freezer for another 3 hours.

Make the final layer by tipping the chopped peaches into a blender with the powdered sugar and white rum. Pulse to make a smooth puree. Take the molds out of the freezer and ladle the mixture into them. Return to the freezer for another 4–5 hours until solid.

CARIBBEAN COCONUT
ICE STICKS

MAKES 10

On the island of Jost Van Dyke, in the Caribbean, there is a beach bar called the Soggy Dollar. Most of its customers are sailors, but there's no dock, so they have to swim ashore and pay for their drinks with wet dollar bills. Apart from being full of waterlogged drinkers, the Soggy Dollar is famous for inventing the Painkiller—a rum and coconut tiki drink that tastes like summer by the sea. This frozen version is based around coconut milk with a dash of dark rum.

½ cup Simple Syrup
(see page 15)
14-oz. can coconut milk
½ cup pineapple juice
½ cup fresh orange juice
2 fl. oz. dark rum

Make the Simple Syrup following the recipe on page 15, then let it cool.

Give the can of coconut milk a good shake to make sure the coconut cream and water are mixed together. Pour into a pitcher. Add the Simple Syrup, pineapple juice, orange juice, and dark rum and stir well. Pour the coconut mixture into molds and freeze for 2–3 hours until slushy and semifrozen. Insert sticks into the ice pops, then freeze overnight until set.

GRAPEFRUIT & BOURBON POPTAILS

MAKES 6–8

The Brown Derby is a cocktail straight out of the 1920s. A simple sour, it's the kind of mixed drink that's easy to turn into an ice pop because the same three elements that make it a great cocktail (sweetness, sourness, and boozy heat) also make it perfect as an ice pop.

• •

1 cup rosemary Simple Syrup (see page 15)
2 cups fresh grapefruit juice
2 fl. oz. bourbon

• •

Make the Simple Syrup following the recipe on page 15, then let it cool.

Pour the grapefruit juice into a pitcher, add the Simple Syrup (strain out the rosemary sprigs) and the bourbon, and stir to mix. Pour the mixture into the molds. Freeze for 2–3 hours, then take the molds out of the freezer and insert the sticks into the slushy, semifrozen ice pops. Freeze for 6–8 hours until solid.

DO-IT-YOURSELF ICE CREAM BARS WITH CHOCOLATE SAUCE

MAKES 8

The kind of DIY I'm happy to get involved in, these luxurious ice pops are made from a quick, no-churn ice cream and served with a warm, boozy chocolate sauce that you can dunk your choc ice into or drizzle over. I like dunking, because the ice pops melt into the sauce, turning it into a lush chocolate pudding.

For the ice cream bars:
14-oz. can sweetened
  condensed milk
1 cup heavy cream
1 cup whole milk
1 tsp. vanilla extract
A pinch of sea salt

For the chocolate sauce:
7 oz. bittersweet chocolate
½ cup heavy cream
2 tbsp. unsalted butter
2 tbsp. maple syrup
2 fl. oz. brandy or dark rum
A pinch of sea salt

To make the ice cream bars, pour the condensed milk and heavy cream into a mixing bowl and whisk together until combined and smooth. Whisk in the milk. Add the vanilla extract and a pinch of salt and whisk again briefly to combine. Use a small ladle to pour the mixture into molds, or transfer the mix to a pitcher and pour. Freeze for 2–3 hours, then insert the sticks and freeze overnight until solid.

Make the chocolate sauce by chopping the chocolate into small chunks and putting them in a heatproof bowl. Set aside. Pour the cream into a saucepan, and add the butter and maple syrup. Set on a low heat and warm the mixture gently until steaming. Pour over the chocolate and stir until the chocolate melts and everything is smoothly combined. Add the brandy or rum and a pinch of salt and stir together. Ladle the warm sauce into small bowls and serve with the ice cream bars. Dip the bars in the sauce, or spoon the sauce over the bars—and watch out for the mess as you eat.

CANTALOUPE COOLERS

MAKES 10

Cantaloupe melons are floral and musky, with a mellow sweetness that pairs beautifully with the sunny smoothness of silver tequila. Add a layer of vanilla-scented Greek yogurt and you've got an ice pop worth lingering over.

½ cup Simple Syrup
(see page 15)
1 cup cantaloupe melon,
chopped
½ cup fresh orange juice
2 fl. oz. silver tequila
1½ cups Greek yogurt
2 tbsp. powdered sugar
1 tsp. vanilla extract

Make the Simple Syrup following the recipe on page 15, then let it cool.

Tip the melon into a blender and add the Simple Syrup, orange juice, and tequila. Blitz until smooth and combined. Pour the melon puree into molds and freeze for 2–3 hours until semifrozen and slushy. Spoon the yogurt into a bowl and add the powdered sugar and vanilla extract. Stir well to mix. Take the molds out of the freezer, spoon in the yogurt mixture, then insert the sticks and freeze overnight until solid.

ESPRESSO MARTINI ICE POPS

MAKES 6

A brunch favorite, Espresso Martinis have the magic effect of waking you up and making you mellow at the same time. These ice pops don't pack quite the same punch, but they would make a great sweet treat after stacks of pancakes on a Sunday morning.

2 tbsp. espresso
2¼ cups whole milk
¾ cup superfine sugar
1 tsp. vanilla extract
2 fl. oz. good-quality vodka

Pour the espresso and milk into a pan. Add the sugar and set the pan on a medium heat. Gently warm, stirring often, until the pan is steaming and just starting to simmer. Turn the heat down and keep it on a gentle simmer for a few minutes, stirring often, until the sugar has dissolved. Set aside to cool (see the tip on page 12 on how to use an ice bath to cool your mixture quickly).

When you're ready to make the ice pops, whisk in the vanilla extract and vodka, then pour the mixture into molds. Freeze for 2–3 hours until semifrozen. Insert sticks into the molds and freeze overnight until solid.

PASSION FRUIT & VODKA RIPPLES

MAKES 4

The inspiration for these indulgent ice pops is the Pornstar Martini, the flamboyant vodka cocktail that comes with a dash of vanilla, half a passion fruit, and a shot of prosecco on the side. Combined with tangy Greek yogurt, the trio of vodka, vanilla, and passion fruit make a not-too-sweet summer treat. Prosecco optional.

Pulp of 3 passion fruits, around 3 oz.
¼ cup powdered sugar
2 fl. oz. good-quality vodka
1½ cups Greek yogurt
1 tsp. vanilla extract

Scoop the passion fruit pulp into a bowl, add the powdered sugar and vodka, and gently stir to mix them together and dissolve the powdered sugar. Add the Greek yogurt and vanilla extract and stir a few times to just mix everything together. Spoon the mixture into ice-pop molds, insert the sticks, and freeze overnight until solid.

PEACH
SANGRIA
ICE POPS

MAKES 6

These pretty ice pops are made with a lighter version of Spanish sangria, using rosé wine and adding a hint of peach. Simmering the mix for a few minutes blends the flavors and also cooks off some of the alcohol, which helps the ice pops freeze.

• •

1⅔ cups rosé wine, such as Zinfandel
1 cup white grape juice
⅓ cup superfine sugar
2 peaches
2 fl. oz. peach schnapps

• •

Pour the wine and grape juice into a saucepan and add the sugar. Set the pan on a medium heat and bring to a gentle boil, stirring to dissolve the sugar. When the pan is just bubbling, turn the heat down and simmer for 5 minutes. Pour the mixture into a pitcher and set aside for 1–2 hours to cool (see the tip on page 12 on using ice baths to cool your ice pop mixes quickly).

When you're ready to freeze the ice pops, halve the peaches and scoop out the pits. Slice the fruit into wedges and drop them into the molds. Stir the peach schnapps into the rosé wine mixture, then pour the mix into molds and freeze for 2–3 hours until slushy and semifrozen. Insert sticks into the molds and freeze overnight until solid.

RUM & BANANA
ICE POPS

MAKES 6

In beach shacks in Jamaica, bartenders shake white rum, coffee liqueur, and crème de banane with cream and milk to make Dirty Bananas—the kind of drink that makes you glad you opted for a vacation full of sun, sea, sand, and cocktails. Turned into an extravagant ice pop, the cocktail tastes innocent but it still packs a boozy punch.

1 cup peeled and sliced bananas
1⅔ cups whole milk
¾ cup powdered sugar
1 fl. oz. crème de banane
½ fl. oz. white rum
½ fl. oz. coffee liqueur

Tip the sliced bananas into a blender and pour in the milk. Add the sugar, the crème de banane, white rum, and coffee liqueur. Blitz until smooth and well combined. Pour the mixture into molds and freeze for 2–3 hours until slushy and semifrozen. Insert sticks into the molds, then freeze overnight until solid.

COSMOPOLITAN PALETAS

MAKES 8

When you're feeling a little Carrie Bradshaw and want to re-create late 90s New York in your kitchen, whip up a batch of these cool and crunchy ice pops. Based on *Sex and the City*'s signature cocktail, they're a stylish mix of tart cranberry juice, smooth vodka, and an orange-scented splash of triple sec. They're the fashion-forward frozen treat of the summer.

1 cup Simple Syrup
   (see page 15)
2 cups cranberry juice
1½ fl. oz. good-quality vodka
½ fl. oz. triple sec
Juice of ½ lime
A few dashes of
   Angostura bitters

Make the Simple Syrup following the recipe on page 15, then let it cool.

Pour the cranberry juice into a pitcher and add the Simple Syrup, vodka, triple sec, lime juice, and a few dashes of Angostura bitters (4–5 good shakes should do it). Stir to mix, then pour the cranberry mixture into the molds. Freeze for 2–3 hours until slushy and semifrozen. Insert sticks into the ice pops. Return to the freezer and freeze overnight until solid.

LIME DAIQUIRI
FREEZER POPS

MAKES 8

A daiquiri is a Cuban cocktail made with white rum, lime juice, and a touch of sugar. This deep-freezer version adds buttermilk into the mix to create smooth, creamy ice pops with a tangy edge.

● ● ● ● ● ● ● ● ● ● ● ● ● ●   ●

1 cup Simple Syrup
  (see page 15)
½ cup fresh lime juice
1¼ cups buttermilk
2 fl. oz. white rum
A few drops of green food
  coloring (optional)

Make the Simple Syrup following the recipe on page 15, then let it cool.

When you're ready to make the ice pops, measure out the Simple Syrup and then add the lime juice, buttermilk, and white rum. Stir to combine. If you want to make the ice pops green, add a few drops of food coloring and stir it in. Pour the mixture into molds and freeze for 2–3 hours until semifrozen. Insert sticks into the ice pops and freeze overnight until solid.

SPICED WHISKEY & FIG CREAM POPS

MAKES 8

This ice pop was inspired by masala chai, the sweet, spicy tea that keeps India running. You need to allow a few hours to infuse the sweetened milk with the spices, and when you're picking a whiskey, go for one that is more nutty and biscuity than smoky.

14-oz. can sweetened condensed milk
1⅔ cups whole milk
4 green cardamom pods
1 star anise
8 cloves
½ tsp. black peppercorns
A slice of fresh ginger
2 fl. oz. good-quality whiskey
2 figs
8 cinnamon sticks (optional)

Pour the condensed milk into a pan. Add the milk and whisk together until smooth. Press the cardamom pods with the flat of a knife to crack them open a little. Add them to the pan with the star anise, cloves, peppercorns, and ginger. Put the pan on a medium heat and bring to a boil, stirring to prevent the mix from sticking and burning. Once the pan starts to bubble, take it off the heat and set aside for 2 hours to cool and infuse.

When you're ready to make the ice pops, strain the milk mixture through a sieve into a pitcher. Stir in the whiskey. Slice the figs into four slices each and pop them in the molds. Pour in the mixture and freeze for 2–3 hours until slushy and semifrozen. Insert cinnamon sticks into the slushy ice pops, if you're using them, or wooden sticks. Return to the freezer and freeze overnight until solid.

RASPBERRY & COCONUT PUNCH POPS

MAKES 6–8

Raspberries and coconut don't get paired up enough. They're a dynamic duo, especially in desserts. These ice pops have a rich coconut base topped with a vodka-spiked raspberry puree that freezes into a mouthwatering treat.

⅔ cup Simple Syrup
    (see page 15)
1½ cups raspberries
Juice of ½ lime
2 fl. oz. good-quality vodka
1 cup coconut milk

Make the Simple Syrup following the recipe on page 15, then let it cool.

Tip the raspberries into a blender. Add half of the Simple Syrup along with the lime juice and vodka and blitz until smooth. Pour the mixture into molds. Freeze for 2–3 hours until just starting to set. Pour the coconut milk into a bowl and add the remaining Simple Syrup to it. Whisk together and pour the coconut mixture into the molds, on top of the semifrozen raspberry mixture. Insert the sticks and freeze overnight until solid.

KIWI CAIPIRINHA COOLERS

MAKES 8

Take your freezer on a trip to Brazil with these ice pops inspired by the famous Latin American drink. The cocktail itself is a simple mix of lime, sugar, and cachaça—a spirit made from sugarcane. To make a longer drink suitable for freezing, I've upped the lime juice and added tart kiwifruits. If you don't have any cachaça, use white rum instead.

1⅓ cups Simple Syrup (see page 15)
2 kiwifruits
½ cup fresh lime juice
⅔ cup cold water
2 fl. oz. cachaça

Make the Simple Syrup following the recipe on page 15, then let it cool.

Slice the skin off the kiwifruits and pop them in a blender. Add the Simple Syrup, lime juice, and water and blitz until smooth. If you'd like clear ice pops, pour the mixture through a sieve into a pitcher to catch any unblended seeds or pulp. Don't press the pulp to squeeze out any remaining juice—that will make the ice pops cloudy. Stir in the cachaça. Pour the mixture into molds. Freeze for 2–3 hours until semifrozen. Insert sticks into the slushy ice pops and freeze overnight until solid.

MELON MOJITO FREEZER POPS

A simple mix of mint, lime, and sugar muddled with rum, cooling mojitos have been enjoyed in Cuba for over 100 years. The final ingredient in the cocktail is soda water, but you need something sweeter to carry the flavors in an ice pop. Galia melon, lush and fragrant, is the perfect stand-in.

• •

1½ cups chopped Galia melon
2 tbsp. superfine sugar
2 sprigs fresh mint, leaves only
Juice of 1 lime
2 fl. oz. white rum

• •

Tip the melon into a blender. Add the sugar, mint leaves, lime juice, and white rum. Blitz until blended and smooth. Pour the mixture into molds and freeze for 2–3 hours until semifrozen. Insert sticks into the molds and freeze overnight until solid.

MERRY BERRY
MULLED WINE
ICE POPS

MAKES 8

Looking for an ice pop for Christmas? Look no further. Mulled wine, full of sugar and spice, is great frozen—especially if you stir in some crushed berries. Choose a juicy red wine, like Merlot, Shiraz, or Gamay, and if you don't like the spices I've suggested, add your own mix. Cardamom pods, peppercorns, fennel seeds, cloves, or strips of orange or lemon peel would all work really well.

1⅔ cups fruity red wine
1 cup fresh orange juice
⅓ cup superfine sugar
1 cinnamon stick
1 star anise
A couple of slices of fresh ginger
1 cup mixed berries, defrosted
    if frozen

Pour the wine and orange juice into a medium saucepan and add the sugar, cinnamon, star anise, and fresh ginger. Set the pan on a medium heat and bring to a gentle boil, stirring to dissolve the sugar. When the liquid is just bubbling, turn the heat down and simmer for 5 minutes. Set aside for 1–2 hours to cool (see the tip on page 12 on using ice baths to cool your ice pop mixes quickly).

When you're ready to freeze the ice pops, place the mixed berries into a bowl and use a fork to roughly crush them. Strain the mulled wine into the bowl with the berries and stir to mix. Ladle the mix into molds and freeze for 2–3 hours until slushy and semifrozen. Insert sticks into the molds and freeze overnight until solid.

ALCOHOL-FREE
ICE POPS

CREAMY CHOCOLATE & BANANA POPS

MAKES 6–8

These ice pops mix the velvety richness of coconut milk and a dark hit of cocoa powder to make freezer pops with a smooth texture and deliciously chocolatey flavor.

● ●

½ cup maple syrup
14-oz. can coconut milk
2 tbsp. unsweetened cocoa powder
A pinch of sea salt
1 small banana

● ●

Pour the syrup into a bowl. Give the can of coconut milk a really good shake to mix the coconut cream and milk together, then pour it into the maple syrup. Add the cocoa powder and a pinch of sea salt and gently whisk until combined. Peel and chop the banana into 20 slices. Drop the banana slices into the ice pop molds, then pour in the coconut mixture. Freeze for 2 hours until semifrozen. Insert sticks into the ice pops, then freeze until solid.

MINT CHOCOLATE CHIP ICE POPS

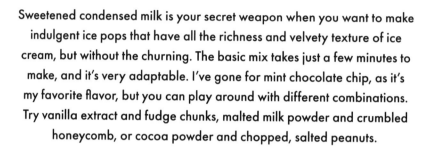

MAKES 10

Sweetened condensed milk is your secret weapon when you want to make indulgent ice pops that have all the richness and velvety texture of ice cream, but without the churning. The basic mix takes just a few minutes to make, and it's very adaptable. I've gone for mint chocolate chip, as it's my favorite flavor, but you can play around with different combinations. Try vanilla extract and fudge chunks, malted milk powder and crumbled honeycomb, or cocoa powder and chopped, salted peanuts.

3 oz. milk chocolate
14-oz. can sweetened condensed milk
1 cup heavy cream
1 cup whole milk
1 tsp. peppermint extract
A few drops of green food coloring (optional)

Grate the chocolate and set it aside for later. Pour the condensed milk and heavy cream into a mixing bowl and whisk together until smooth. Whisk in the milk. Add the peppermint extract and a few drops of green food coloring, if using, then whisk again briefly to combine. Use a small ladle to pour the mixture into molds, or transfer the mix to a pitcher and pour it in. Freeze for 2–3 hours until slushy. Divide the grated chocolate between the molds, and gently stir with a butter knife or skewer. Insert the sticks and freeze overnight until solid.

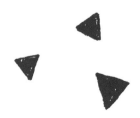

POPTAIL IT

For an adults-only version of this ice pop, swap the peppermint extract for 1 fl. oz. crème de menthe.

CHOCOLATE CHERRY RIPPLES

MAKES 6

An ice pop of two halves, both featuring juicy fresh cherries.
The bottom layer is a classic mix of Greek yogurt and honey,
while the top has a bittersweet swirl of cocoa powder
stirred through it.

• • • • • • • • • • • • •   •

1¼ cups Greek yogurt
1¼ cups whole milk
¼ cup honey
1 heaping tbsp. unsweetened
   cocoa powder
¾ cup fresh cherries, halved
   and pitted

Spoon half the yogurt into a mixing bowl, then add
half the milk and half the honey and whisk together.
Tip in the cocoa powder and use a spatula to fold
everything together. Ladle the chocolate mixture into the
ice pop molds, filling them so they are half to three-
quarters full. Drop in a few cherry halves. Slide the
molds into the freezer and freeze for 2 hours.

When the ice pops are just starting to set, whisk the
remaining yogurt, milk, and honey together in a bowl.
Spoon it into the molds, drop in a few more cherry
halves, insert the sticks, and freeze for another 5–6 hours
or overnight until solid.

PINK LEMONADE
ICE POPS

MAKES 8

Take a trip back to your childhood with these nostalgic ice pops. They get their pale pink color from a handful of strawberries blitzed with simple syrup and fresh lemon juice. The mixture will taste very sweet when you make it, but once it's frozen the sugar balances out with the sharp lemon juice to make a refreshing treat.

1⅓ cups Simple Syrup (see page 15)
½ cup strawberries
1 cup fresh lemon juice
⅔ cup cold water

Make the Simple Syrup following the recipe on page 15, then let it cool.

Hull the strawberries and pop them in a blender. Add the Simple Syrup, lemon juice, and water and blitz until smooth. If you'd like clear ice pops, pour the mixture through a sieve to catch any unblended seeds or pulp. Don't press the pulp to squeeze out any remaining juice—that will make the ice pops cloudy.

Pour the mixture into molds. Freeze for 2–3 hours until just starting to freeze, then insert sticks into the slushy ice pops and freeze for another 6–8 hours until solid.

POPTAIL IT
Add 2 fl. oz. vodka to the mixture for strawberry vodka ice pops, then freeze overnight.

BERRY BREAKFAST YOGURT POPS

MAKES 6-8

The ingredients in these yogurt pops—yogurt, milk, honey, berries, and granola—are no different from your regular breakfast bowl. They're just a lot more fun to eat when they're served on a stick.

1 cup mixed berries, such as strawberries, blueberries, and raspberries
1¼ cups Greek yogurt
1 cup whole milk
¼ cup honey
⅔ cup granola

If you're using strawberries, hull them, then thinly slice or roughly chop them. Spoon the yogurt into a mixing bowl, then add the milk and honey. Whisk together until smooth and combined. Stir in the berries. Spoon the mixture into the molds, leaving a small gap at the top of each mold, around ¾ inch, then sprinkle over the granola evenly. Insert a stick into each mold and freeze overnight.

EASY WATERMELON FREEZER POPS

MAKES 5–10

This recipe is so simple it isn't really a recipe at all. But when summer is here, hot and blazing, you'll be glad you have a stack of these watermelon wedges in your freezer. They take a few minutes to assemble and, eaten straight from the freezer, they have a crunchy, almost granita-like texture. If you don't mind sticky fingers, squeeze a little lime juice over them just before eating. It brings out the melon's sweetness.

A wedge of watermelon

POPTAIL IT
Pour a large measure of ice-cold vodka into tumblers and place a watermelon pop in each glass to serve.

Line a cookie sheet with parchment paper. Slice the watermelon into triangle-shaped pieces around ¾–1 inch thick. Insert a small, sharp knife into the rind in the middle of each wedge to create a little opening.

Insert a stick into each opening, then place the watermelon slices on the sheet. Slide into the freezer and freeze overnight. Wrap the watermelon pops in waxed paper or freezer wrap, and store them in a freezerproof tub.

These pops are best eaten within one week of making.

MANGO & YOGURT TWISTS

MAKES 6

Cheerful swirls of lime-spiked mango mingle with thick spoonfuls
of just-sweet-enough yogurt to make an ice pop that would be perfect
served as dessert after a dinner that is full of spice and chili heat.

● ●

9 oz. mango pulp or chopped
   fresh mango
¼ cup powdered sugar
Juice of ½ lime
1½ cups Greek yogurt
1 tsp. vanilla extract

If you're using chopped fresh mango, pop it into a small
bowl and puree it with a handheld blender, or blitz in a
blender until smooth. Add half of the powdered sugar
and all of the lime juice to the pulp and either blitz again
or use a spoon to beat it in. Spoon the yogurt into a
separate bowl and add the remaining powdered sugar
and the vanilla extract. Stir well to mix.

Spoon the yogurt and the mango pulp into your molds
in alternate layers until you've used them all up. Gently
stir a butter knife or skewer through the yogurt and
mango a few times to swirl them together. Insert sticks
into the ice pops and freeze overnight until solid.

APRICOT & BAY PALETAS

MAKES 6-8

In Mexico, paletas are ice pops typically made with fresh fruit, and the flavors change with the season. These glossy apricot ice pops taste like early summer on a stick. When fresh apricots aren't available, you can use two 14-oz. cans of apricots in fruit juice, drained, instead.

• •

2 cups fresh apricots, halved
    and pitted
1 large bay leaf
¾ cup superfine sugar
⅔ cup cold water
Juice of ½ lemon

Place the apricots in a saucepan and add the bay leaf, sugar, and water. Set the pan on a medium heat, pop on a lid, and bring to a gentle boil. When the mixture is just bubbling, turn the heat down a little and simmer for 5–10 minutes until the apricots break down and become soft and pulpy. Set aside to cool (see the tip on page 12 on using ice baths to cool your ice-pop mixes quickly).

When you're ready to make the paletas, pick out the bay leaf and discard it. Stir in the lemon juice. Use a handheld blender to blitz the apricots into a smooth puree, or ladle everything into a blender and blitz. Pour the mixture into molds and freeze for 2–3 hours until semifrozen. Insert sticks and freeze overnight until solid.

CHOCOLATE BANANA
FREEZER POPS

MAKES 8

These easy banana pops can be as grown-up or as crazy as you like. Dipped in bittersweet chocolate and sprinkled with chopped hazelnuts and a little sea salt, they're a sophisticated dessert (kind of). Dip the bananas in milk chocolate and coat them with mini marshmallows, caramel shards, and pretzel pieces and they're the sort of thing kids—and parents—will love.

4 bananas

4½ oz. bittersweet or milk chocolate

1 tbsp. vegetable oil

A few tbsp. of toppings, such as sprinkles, dried coconut, or chopped nuts

*TOP TIP:

For a faster melt, use a microwave set to high and stir every 15 seconds—it's very easy to burn chocolate in a microwave, so watch it carefully.

Line a cookie sheet with parchment paper. Halve the bananas and insert a stick into the cut end of each half. Lay them on the tray and freeze for 30 minutes.

While the bananas freeze, half-fill a pan with water, set it on a high heat, and bring it to a rolling boil. Snap the chocolate into small pieces and pop them in a heatproof bowl with the vegetable oil. Set the bowl over the pan of water, making sure the bowl doesn't touch the water. Turn the heat off and let the chocolate slowly melt, stirring it occasionally. This will take around 20–30 minutes.*

Tip any toppings you are going to use into small bowls, so they're easy to reach. Take the semifrozen bananas out of the freezer. Hold one frozen banana half over the bowl of chocolate and spoon over the melted chocolate to lightly coat it. Lay the banana back down on the cookie sheet and sprinkle with your choice of topping (the chocolate will begin to set straight away, so you need to sprinkle over the toppings as soon as each banana half is coated). Repeat to use all the bananas, chocolate, and toppings.

Freeze again for around 1 hour, then serve or transfer to a freezerproof tub, layering the pops with sheets of waxed paper. These freezer pops are best eaten within one week of making.

WATERMELON
PALETAS

MAKES 6

Paleterías in Mexico specialize in paletas (ice pops) made from fresh, seasonal ingredients. I've followed their lead and kept these ice pops simple: plenty of juicy watermelon, a squeeze of lime to bring out the flavor, and a touch of sugar.

16 oz. chopped watermelon, rind removed
Juice of 1 lime
2 tbsp. superfine sugar
Lime or lemon juice and sea salt, to serve

Flick as many of the black seeds out of the watermelon as possible, then tip the chunks of fruit into a blender. Add the lime juice and sugar. Blitz to make a smooth puree. For clear paletas, pour the puree through a sieve into a pitcher to catch any unblended seeds or pulp. Don't press the fruit in the sieve to extract more juice — that will make the paletas cloudy. Pour the watermelon mixture into molds and freeze for 2–3 hours until slushy and semifrozen. Insert the wooden sticks into the molds, then freeze overnight until solid.

A fun way to serve these paletas is in a glass with a rim dipped in lime or lemon juice and then in sea salt to lightly coat. You can let them melt, or drag the paleta through the salt for a savory tang.

POPTAIL IT

Turn these paletas into an adults-only treat by adding a shot of chilled tequila and triple sec to the glass, and tucking in half a jalapeño for a kick of chili heat.

BLUEBERRY CHEESECAKE POPS

MAKES 5

The mix of Greek yogurt and cream cheese in these cheesecake pops gives them a tart and tangy flavor that's sweetened by a little honey. I've left it up to you how much honey to add; go for less if you want the sharpness of the blueberries to shine through, or add more for a richer, more luscious flavor. Whatever you do, don't skip the salt. It adds a savory note that in a slice of cheesecake would come from the crust.

½ cup blueberries
1 cup Greek yogurt
1 cup full-fat cream cheese
2–4 tbsp. honey
Juice of ½ lime
A pinch of sea salt

Chop the blueberries. Spoon the yogurt and cream cheese into a mixing bowl. Add the honey (use 2 tablespoons for a tart flavor, 4 tablespoons for something sweeter), the lime juice, and a pinch of sea salt. Whisk together until smooth and combined. Add the blueberries and use a spoon to fold them into the mixture. Use a small spoon to divide the mixture between molds. Insert the sticks and freeze overnight.

FRESH ORANGE
ICE POPS

MAKES 6–8

Ice pops made with fresh juices have a brighter, more mouthwatering flavor than anything you can buy from the store. Once you have mastered these easy-to-make orange ice pops (one go should do it!), you can experiment with swapping the orange juice for your favorite fruit juice, such as grapefruit, apple, or cranberry.

1 cup Simple Syrup
  (see page 15)
½ orange
2 cups fresh orange juice

Make the Simple Syrup following the recipe on page 15, then let it cool.

Slice the orange half into thin slices. Pop one slice into each mold. Pour the orange juice into a pitcher and add the Simple Syrup. Stir to mix, then pour the orange mixture into the molds. Freeze for 2–3 hours, then take the molds out of the freezer and insert the sticks into the slushy, semifrozen ice pops. Return to the freezer and freeze for 3–5 hours until solid.

POPTAIL IT

Turn these ice pops into Screwdriver pops by adding 2 fl. oz. good-quality vodka and a few dashes of Angostura bitters with the Simple Syrup.

AVOCADO &
COCONUT ICE STICKS

MAKES 8

Buttery avocados are amazing in ice pops. They have a luxurious texture that's just as good as cream or yogurt for creating a rich, luscious consistency. These avocado and coconut ice sticks are balanced between sweet and savory, so they feel indulgent and a bit good for you, too.

2 ripe avocados (weighing around 14 oz., including skin and pits)
1 cup coconut milk
2 tbsp. maple or agave syrup
Juice of ½ lime
A pinch of sea salt
3–4 tbsp. cold water (optional)

Halve the avocados, remove the pits, then scoop the flesh into a blender. If the coconut milk is in a can, give it a really good shake to mix the coconut cream and milk together, then measure out 1 cup and add it to the blender. Add the maple or agave syrup, lime juice, and a pinch of sea salt. Blitz until smooth and combined. If the mixture seems a bit thick, add some or all of the water and blitz again. Pour the mixture into molds, insert the sticks, and freeze overnight until firm.

POPTAIL IT
If you'd like to turn these ice sticks into grown-up treats, add 2 fl. oz. white or coconut rum.

COCONUT
COOLERS

MAKES 5

These creamy coconut ice pops come with a dash of lime.
They're easy to make and a quicker way to take yourself
to the Caribbean than getting on a plane.

½ cup Simple Syrup
   (see page 15)
14-oz. can coconut milk
Juice of 1 lime
A few pinches of flaked
   coconut

Make the Simple Syrup following the recipe on page 15, then let it cool.

Give the can of coconut milk a good shake to make sure the coconut cream and milk are mixed together. Pour into a pitcher. Add the simple syrup and lime juice and stir well. Pour the coconut mixture into the molds and freeze for 2–3 hours until slushy and semifrozen. Sprinkle a few pinches of flaked coconut into the molds, insert sticks into the ice pops, then freeze overnight until solid.

TIRAMISU
PICK-ME-UPS

MAKES 10

In a restaurant in northern Italy in the 1960s, a pastry chef layered up ladyfingers, mascarpone, cream, and a dusting of cocoa powder and he called it *tiramisù*. The name translates from Italian as "pick me up," and the pudding does perk up anyone who eats it. Not just because of the coffee or the cheering effects of a bowlful of cream and chocolate, but because tiramisu is said to be an aphrodisiac. I can't promise these portable tiramisus will win over the object of your affection, but they will definitely be impressed by your ice pop–making skills, which has to count for something, right?

● ●

1 oz. bittersweet chocolate

½ cup mascarpone

14-oz. can sweetened condensed milk

1⅓ cups heavy cream

1 tsp. unsweetened cocoa powder

2 tbsp. espresso, cooled

1 tsp. vanilla extract

10 ladyfingers

POPTAIL IT

Follow the original dessert and add 1 fl. oz. coffee liqueur with the cocoa powder and espresso, and 1 fl. oz. brandy with the vanilla extract.

Coarsely grate the chocolate and set aside. Spoon the mascarpone into a mixing bowl and beat until smooth and creamy. Slowly whisk in the condensed milk until it is evenly combined, then add the cream and whisk that in, too. Ladle half the mix into a separate bowl.

Add the cocoa powder and the espresso to one of the bowls and whisk them together. Stir in half the grated chocolate. To the other bowl, add the vanilla extract. Whisk to combine. Cover the vanilla mixture with plastic wrap and store it in your fridge for later. Use a small ladle to pour the chocolatey mixture into the molds to half-fill them—these ice pops are best made in rigid plastic molds—or transfer the mix to a pitcher to pour in. Break up a ladyfinger and tuck into each mold. Pop the ice pops into the freezer for 2–3 hours until semifrozen.

Take the molds out of the freezer and spoon in the vanilla mix to fill them. Sprinkle the remaining chocolate over the ice pops. Insert the sticks and freeze overnight until solid.

EASY COLA
ICE POPS

MAKES 6–8

Cola is great frozen; the sweetness becomes refreshing,
and adding a sharp dash of lime brings out the aromatic spices.

2¾ cups cola
½ lemon
½ lime
Juice of 1 lime

Pour the cola into a pitcher and let it sit for 1–2 hours to go slightly flat. Finely slice the lemon and lime halves, then drop a slice of each into each ice-pop mold. Add the lime juice to the cola. Stir together, then pour into the molds and freeze for 2–3 hours until slushy and semifrozen. Insert sticks and freeze overnight until solid.

POPTAIL IT
Turn these ice pops into frozen Cuba Libres by adding 2 fl. oz. white rum with the lime juice, and a few dashes of Angostura bitters.

PINEAPPLE & COCONUT CREAM POPS

MAKES 10

The mix of coconut and pineapple gives these ice pops a soft, fluffy texture. They were inspired by Puerto Rico's national drink, the piña colada. For a tipsy version of these ice pops, add 2 fl. oz. white rum to the mix.

• •

½ cup Simple Syrup (see page 15)
14-oz. can pineapple chunks in juice
14-oz. can coconut milk
Juice of 1 lime
1½ tbsp. coconut cream

• •

Make the Simple Syrup following the recipe on page 15, then let it cool.

Tip the can of pineapple and its juice into a blender. Pour in the coconut milk, Simple Syrup, and lime juice. Crumble in the coconut cream and blitz until combined. Pour the mixture into molds and freeze for 2–3 hours until thickened. Insert sticks and freeze overnight until solid.

CHOCOLATE & HAZELNUT POPS

MAKES 10

In these intensely rich chocolate ice pops, a scoop of chocolate hazelnut spread adds praline nuttiness to the quick and easy ice cream mix, while a handful of chopped hazelnuts sprinkled over just before serving adds crunch. For extra richness, toast the hazelnuts before chopping.

● ● ● ● ● ● ● ● ● ● ● ● ● ● ● ●   ●

½ cup chocolate hazelnut spread
1 cup heavy cream
1 cup whole milk
14-oz. can sweetened
   condensed milk
A pinch of sea salt
Chopped hazelnuts, to serve

Scoop the chocolate hazelnut spread into your blender, then pour in the cream and milk. Blitz until well mixed. Scoop in the condensed milk and add a pinch of sea salt. Blitz again until smooth and creamy. Ladle the mixture into molds, or transfer it into a pitcher to make it easy to pour. Freeze for 2–3 hours, until slushy, then insert the sticks and freeze overnight until set.

To serve, unmold the pops and sprinkle with a few chopped hazelnuts. You can refreeze the pops once you've added the hazelnuts to set them—see the tip on page 13 on setting and storing your pops.

136

PERSIMMON SORBET SHOTS

MAKES 8

These fruity ice pops are sorbet on a stick. Made with honey-fleshed persimmons blitzed with a little sugar and fresh citrus, they have a velvety texture and a sweet, sherbetty flavor.

• •

10½ oz. ripe persimmons, roughly chopped
2 heaping tbsp. superfine sugar
⅔ cup fresh clementine juice
Juice of ½ lime

• •

Tip the chopped persimmons into a blender and add the sugar, clementine juice, and lime juice. Blitz until blended and smooth. Pour the mixture into shot glasses or molds (don't be tempted to strain it through a sieve— the pulp gives the ice pops their soft, silky texture), then insert sticks and freeze overnight until solid.

STRAWBERRIES & CREAM
ICE POPS

MAKES 10–12

Like a strawberry milkshake that's taken a trip to Siberia, these quick, creamy ice pops have a fluffy texture and a tasty berry sweetness.

½ cup Simple Syrup
   (see page 15)
½ cup strawberries
14-oz. can sweetened
   condensed milk
1 cup heavy cream
1 cup whole milk
1 tsp. vanilla extract

Make the Simple Syrup following the recipe on page 15, then let it cool.

Hull and chop the strawberries. Tip them into your blender, add the Simple Syrup, and blitz until you have a smooth puree. Scoop the condensed milk into the blender, then pour in the cream, milk, and vanilla extract. Pulse a few times to lightly mix everything together. Pour the mixture into molds and freeze for 2–3 hours until semifrozen. Insert sticks into the molds and freeze overnight until set.

INDEX